First Grade

Now I Know

Horses

Written by Rose Greydanus
Illustrated by Joel Snyder

Troll Associates

Library of Congress Cataloging in Publication Data

Greydanus, Rose.
  Horses.

  (Now I know)
  Summary: Simple text and illustrations introduce the
characteristics of horses.
  1. Horses—Juvenile literature. [1. Horses]
I. Snyder, Joel, ill. II. Title
SF302.G73 1983   636.1   82-20296
ISBN 0-89375-900-7

10   9   8   7   6   5   4   3   2   1

Horses are beautiful animals.

They are very strong, too.

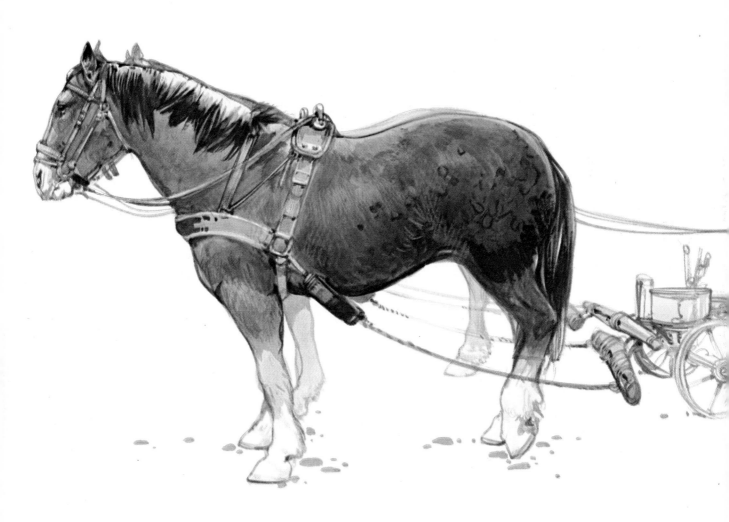

In the past, horses did hard work.

Today, horses are for riding
and jumping and running!

Horses can run very fast.

They have long strong legs.

Their feet, or hoofs, are hard.

Horses have long tails.

Their tails are good for many things!

A horse's body is covered with short hair.

But it has long hair on its head and neck
called a *mane*.

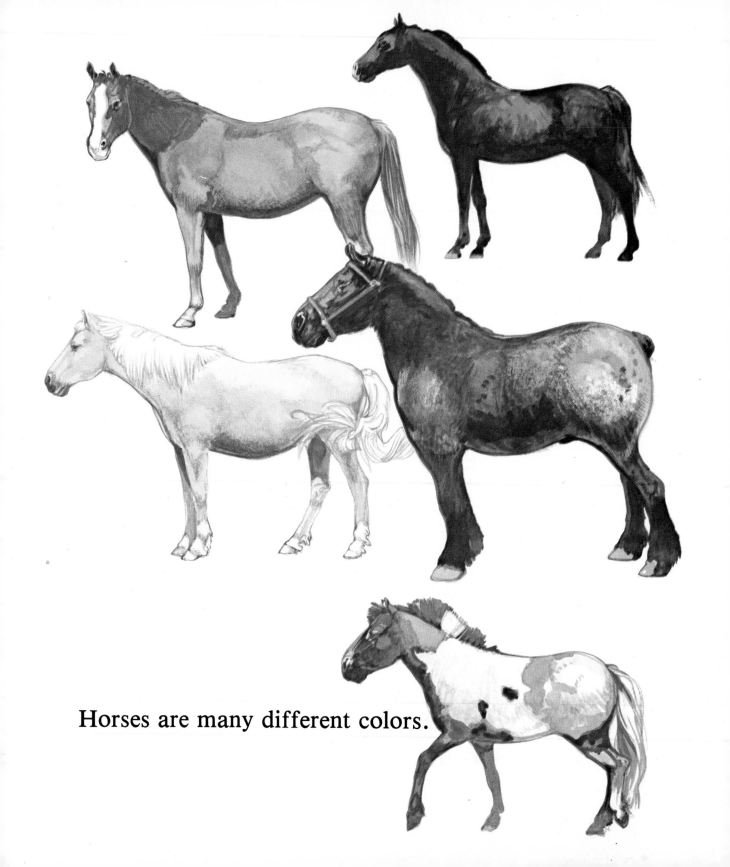

Horses are many different colors.

This beautiful *palomino* has golden hair
and a white mane.

And here is a black and white spotted *pinto*.

A pony is a short horse.

This is a *Shetland* pony.

Shetland ponies are very kind and gentle.

A baby horse is called a *foal*.

When a foal is first born,
its long legs shake and wobble.

But soon, it is running with its mother.

Most horses are full grown when
they are 5 years old.

They eat a lot of food.

They like to eat grass and hay.

But most of all, they like to eat oats!

After a long day of running and jumping...

...this foal

and its mother are ready to sleep.

Good Night!